Arts and Music

Dan Lyndon-Cohen

FRANKLIN WATTS
LONDON • SYDNEY

This edition 2020

First published in 2010 by Franklin Watts

Copyright © The Watts Publishing Group 2010

Editor: Tracey Kelly
Series editor: Adrian Cole
Art director: Jonathan Hair
Design: Stephen Prosser
Picture research: Diana Morris

Dan Lyndon-Cohen would like to thank the following people for their support in writing this book; The Black and Asian Studies Association (BASA), Marika Sherwood, Arthur Torrington, Joanna Cohen and Joanna Caroussis. Thanks also to the Lyndon, Robinson, Cohen and Childs families.

This series is dedicated to the memory of Kodjo Yenga.

Acknowledgements:

Ana Abejon/istockphoto: front cover r, back cover l. Janette Beckmann/Getty Images: 36bl. Ron Burton/Keystone/Getty Images: 23bl. Paul Carstairs/Alamy: 23tr. Cheryl Casey/Shutterstock: 10 background. E. Dean/Topical Press Agency/Getty Images: 31b. Mary Evans PL: 10b, 15t, 18t. The Granger Collection/Topfoto: 8, 13tr, 14,19t, 20, 21t, 21b, 24b, 24b inset. Hulton Archive/Getty Images: 12c, 22b. David Huntley/Shutterstock: 22 background. Chris Jackson/Getty Images: 39tr. Amy Johansson/Shutterstock: 12 background. Cambridge Jones/Getty Images: 33b. John Keith/Shutterstock: 6. Jak Kilby/Arenapal/Topfoto: 11t. Leenvdb/Shutterstock: endpapers. Martin McNeil/Wirelmage/Getty mages: 38. Etham Miller/Getty Images: 36cr. MPI/Getty Images: 29t. Naki/Redferns/Getty Images: 37. The National Archives/HIP/Topfoto: 16. Michael Ochs Collection/Getty Images: 9t, 9b, 29b. Pictorial Press/Alamy: 17, 26, 27. Vasily Pindyurin/Shutterstock: 28 background. David Redfern/Getty Images: 28c. Ebet Roberts/Redferns/Getty Images: 35t. Paul Salmon/Alamy: 39bl. Paul Seuxe/Hemis/Alamy: 11b. Herb Snitzer/Arenapal/Topfoto: front cover l, back cover r. SSPL/Getty Images: 33t. Homer Sykes/Alamy: 34. Topfoto: 25, 30. Ann Trilling/Shutterstock: 18 background. Ullsteinbild/Topfoto: 5, 31t. Noel Vasquez/Getty Images: 35b. V & A Images/Alamy: 15b. Rob Verhorst/Redferns/Getty Images: 32. Michael Ward/Rex Features: 19b.

Every attempt has been made to clear copyright.
Should there be any inadvertent omission please apply to the publisher for rectification.

PB ISBN: 978 1 4451 8078 6
eBook ISBN: 978 1 4451 8079 3

Printed in Dubai

Franklin Watts is a division of Hachette Children's Books, an Hachette UK company.
Carmelite House
50 Victoria Embankment
London, EC4Y 0DZ
www.hachette.co.uk

Contents

Introduction

Whether you enjoy listening to music, reading books and poetry, watching films or visiting art museums, the contributions made by artists and performers of African origin are all around you. Rising out of the shackles of slavery in centuries past to increased recognition in this new century, it is clear that black people have made an enormous contribution to culture around the world.

Musical roots

Jazz and the blues trace their origins back to the sounds of enslaved Africans, who created music as a form of resistance against slavery in the Americas. During the early 20th century, jazz and blues evolved and were played across the USA, from the backwaters of the Mississippi Delta, to the clubs in cities such as Chicago and New York, until their sounds spread across the globe. In 21st-century Britain and the USA, you might hear the heavy bass lines of the latest dubstep track, which is influenced by reggae of the 1970s, or the latest hip hop, influenced by the West African griots (see pages 10–11).

▲ *This wood engraving shows former slaves singing outside a farm building in 1876.*

Art and literature

Today, it is impossible not to recognise the contribution made to the world of art and literature by black men and women, but the struggle to be recognised continues into the 21st century. You've probably watched films starring Samuel L. Jackson or Will Smith, but have you seen the art of Chris Ofili? Maybe you have read some of the books by Maya Angelou and Malorie Blackman, but what about Zadie Smith? Everyone knows the songs of Michael Jackson and Tina Turner, but have you heard the reggae of Bob Marley, songs by Duke Ellington (see right), or the performance poetry of Benjamin Zephaniah? All over the world black men and women are contributing to a vibrant cultural experience.

▲ *The Jackson 5 in 1973. (From left) Tito, Marlon, Jackie, Michael and Jermaine.*

What's inside?

There's only so much you can squeeze into one book. But here there is a glimpse at the history of modern music, and the ways in which black people have been portrayed in art. You will also find out how black writers contributed to civil rights campaigns, and how black actors have expressed the emotions and thoughts of their time. This is a story of creativity and a powerful struggle to be heard, read and seen.

The Duke

Known as a great genius of jazz, Duke Ellington (1899–1974) was a bandleader, pianist and composer. He worked for 60 years in orchestral jazz, big band and swing, as well as blues, gospel, film soundtracks and classical music. He also appeared in several films – the first being *Black and Tan* in 1929. In the 1920s, Ellington's band presided over the Cotton Club, a nightclub in Harlem, New York, and in the 1930s and 40s, he had huge hits such as *Mood Indigo* and *Take the 'A' Train*.

▲ *Duke Ellington at the piano, c.1940. He received a Grammy Lifetime Achievement award in 1966.*

The music of Africa

The rhythms of Africa have had a great influence on modern music. According to Olaudah Equiano (an enslaved African who published his autobiography, *The Interesting Narrative ...*, to support the fight against slavery), the people of West Africa have always had a strong musical heritage: *"Every great event, such as a triumphant return from battle, or other cause of public rejoicing, is celebrated in public dances, which are accompanied with songs and music suited to the occasion."*

Ceremonial music

In countries such as Equiano's 18th-century Benin, music was played at different occasions and served many purposes. There were formal events, such as the crowning of a new king, with hundreds of musicians, singers and dancers taking part. Or when the men of the tribe went off hunting, music would be played to send them on their way. Music was also part of events such as giving birth, which would often be sung by women only. European travellers to West Africa often remarked that music was an important part of daily village life, with songs about farming, going to the market and preparing food.

▲ *Dance and music were very much part of African life. Here the King of Benin is crowned in 1725.*

African instruments

Equiano also described the different musical instruments that were played:

> "...particularly drums of different kinds, a piece of music which resembles a guitar, and another much like a stickado (a thumb piano)."

▲ The thumb piano, called a mbira, is the national instrument of Zimbabwe.

Drumming in African music is hugely important. There were many types of drum, ranging in size (and sound) from drums that were 25 centimetres wide, to enormous drums 10 metres wide! The drum skins were made from animal skins, with the most important drums being covered in leopard skin. Other instruments included percussion such as bells, gongs and rattles; wind instruments such as pipes, horns and flutes; and stringed instruments such as lutes and fiddles.

Travelling griots

In many West African communities, singers and storytellers known as griots sang songs about the history and culture of their tribe, to praise their leaders and pass on stories from generation to generation. Griots were expected to extemporise, which means that they had to make up the words and music as they went along. This was a bit like a modern day 'Emcee battle', where rappers compete to see who can come up with the best lyrics. The griots have also been linked to the development of blues music, which combined a vocal solo (like the griots) with the melody (from the 'field hollers' of the slaves) and the rhythm (from work songs sung by slaves).

▲ This griot is from modern-day Mali and has a home-made guitar-like instrument.

The impact of slavery

From the 16th to 19th centuries, the Transatlantic Slave Trade resulted in millions of Africans being transported to the Americas. Africans brought with them many traditions including music, dance and storytelling, which they tried to keep alive. Some of these influences became very important, especially in music, and led to the development of forms that still influence music today. Many important writers who had been enslaved influenced not only the campaign to abolish slavery, but also left their mark on modern literature.

Spirituals and hollers

Life on the slave plantations was incredibly hard. Africans often sang songs while working to keep their spirits up, and as a form of resistance against the slave owners. Drumming was even banned in some of the Southern states as it was feared that drums could be sending a message to other slaves to overthrow their owners.

The songs that were sung in the fields and at church were a mixture of 'spirituals', which had a religious message, and 'hollers', sung by individuals. Some of the songs carried secret messages about escaping from slavery, including the song *Swing Low, Sweet Chariot* (now connected with the English Rugby Union team!). It is thought that the blues developed from the hollers and griots (see pages 10–11) and that jazz grew from a different style, known as the 'shout'.

▲ *The tradition of enslaved Africans singing 'spirituals' and 'hollers' continued into the early 20th century.*

Unique literature

It was very unusual for enslaved Africans to be able to read and write, because their owners thought it was either a waste of time or too risky – keeping slaves illiterate was a way of controlling them. However, literate slaves were able to take on positions of responsibility and some used their skills to write about their experiences.

Probably the most famous were Olaudah Equiano, who published his autobiography *The Interesting Narrative of Gustavus Vassa, or Olaudah Equiano* in 1789, and Mary Prince, who published *The History of Mary Prince: A West Indian Slave* in 1831. Both were used in the campaign to abolish slavery.

Phillis Wheatley

A former slave named Phillis Wheatley became the first African American to have a book published when her *Poems on Various Subjects, Religious and Moral* was printed in 1773. Included were beautiful tributes to friends who had died:

"From dark abodes to fair ethereal light
Th' enraptur'd innocent has wing'd her flight;
On the kind bosom of eternal love
She finds unknown beatitude above..."

▶ *Phillis Wheatley (c. 1753–1784).*

At first, many people did not believe a black woman was capable of writing poetry, and so Wheatley had to prove her ability in the US court. The book was eventually published in England and was praised by US President George Washington and other important figures.

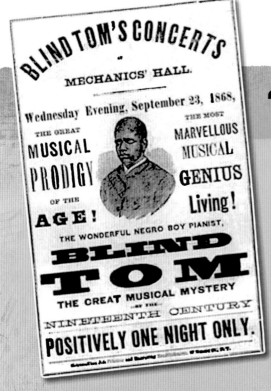

▲ *A poster from 1868 advertising a Blind Tom concert.*

'Blind Tom' Bethune

'Blind Tom' Bethune performed during the late 19th century. Tom was sold into slavery with his parents and was bought by James Bethune in 1851. He was blind and autistic but had incredible talent on the piano – he could listen to a piece of music and play it back after just one hearing. Once his owner realised how talented Tom was, he took him on tours across the USA. He even played for President James Buchanan in 1860. Tom earned his owner over $100,000, but he and his family received almost nothing for his talents.

The actor – Ira Aldridge

In 1807, the year that the slave trade was abolished in Britain, one of the greatest African-American actors of the 19th century was born in the USA. However, Ira Aldridge was not able to perform in the country of his birth because of racist attitudes there, so he travelled to Britain to act. Aldridge also toured across Europe, winning praise and awards throughout his career. In 1863, he became a British citizen, having married an English woman, Margaret Gill, in 1824.

The early years

Although Aldridge was believed to have been born in New York, some stories have suggested that he was born in Africa, the son of a prince. His father became a preacher and it seemed that Ira would follow in his father's footsteps. But while attending the Afro-American Free School and spending time at the local Park Theater, he discovered a love of acting.

Ira began working backstage for an English actor, James Wallack, and in 1824, he travelled with him to England, realising it would be very difficult for a black actor to find work in the USA while slavery still existed. After a fall out with Wallack, Aldridge headed for London and ended up working as an actor at the Coburg Theatre (now called the 'Old Vic'), where he began performing.

The African Roscius

Aldridge made his debut at the Coburg in October 1825, becoming the first black actor to perform at the theatre. His debut role was Oroonoko, an African prince. At first, he received a hostile response from the critics, some of whom made racist comments. However, the audiences were much more positive. Aldridge became best known for his portrayal of the title role in Shakespeare's *Othello*, and in 1833, he performed this at the Theatre Royal in Covent Garden, one of the most famous theatres in London.

▲ *This portrait of Ira Aldridge as Othello was painted by H. P. Briggs, c.1830.*

▲ *This is the Theatre Royal, Covent Garden, London, in 1810.*

Aldridge became known as the 'African Roscius', a reference to a Roman slave who became a famous actor during the time of Julius Caesar. Aldridge embarked on a tour of Britain after some London newspapers criticised the fact that a black actor was working with white actresses. One even wrote that he had concerns about one actress being "pawed about on the stage by a black man".

European star

By the 1850s, Aldridge's reputation was strong enough for him to be able to tour across Europe, where he became one of the most celebrated actors of the age. He was even given medals by the King of Prussia and the Emperor of Austria. In Russia, he performed for the Tsar (Emperor) and was paid £60 for every performance. This made him one of the highest paid actors in the world. His Shakespearean

roles expanded to include not only Othello, but also Shylock in *The Merchant of Venice*, Macbeth, King Lear and Hamlet; he was the first black actor to play these parts. A critic from Austria wrote that, "Ira Aldridge is without a doubt the greatest actor that has ever been seen in Europe".

▲ *Ira Aldridge as Othello c.1848. Aldridge carried on acting until his death in 1867.*

The composer – Samuel Coleridge-Taylor

IN DEPTH

Just as the American actor Ira Aldridge found fame across the Atlantic Ocean, his musical counterpart, the composer Samuel Coleridge-Taylor, found success abroad too. Coleridge-Taylor was also a political activist who was involved in the 1900 Pan-African Conference, which brought together delegates from Britain, the USA, the Caribbean and Africa to fight for equal rights for Africans.

▲ *Samuel Coleridge-Taylor faced racism in Britain, and found the USA more welcoming.*

The early years

Samuel Coleridge-Taylor was born in London in 1875. His father, Daniel Taylor, was a doctor from Sierra Leone and his mother, Alice Hare, was a white woman. Daniel Taylor struggled to find work in London as many hospitals refused to hire black doctors, and so he returned to Sierra Leone, and Coleridge-Taylor was brought up by his mother and stepfather. Their home was very musical and he learned to play the violin, eventually earning a place at the Royal College of Music (RCM) at the age of 15. Here, he was taught to compose by Sir Charles Villiers Stanford, a famous professor and composer.

The Hiawatha trilogy

After graduating from the RCM, Coleridge-Taylor collaborated with an African-American poet named Paul Laurence Dunbar, putting his poetry to music in a piece called *Seven African Romances*. However, his most famous work was a

trilogy of pieces based around 'Hiawatha', a poem by Henry Longfellow. Coleridge-Taylor wrote *Hiawatha's Wedding Feast* in 1898, *The Death of Minnehaha* in 1899 and *Hiawatha's Departure* in 1900. *Hiawatha's Wedding Feast* was especially popular – it was performed many times in Britain and the USA, and is still performed today.

▲ *Samuel Coleridge-Taylor at his piano, with a copy of the music for* Hiawatha's Wedding Feast.

Roots music

Coleridge-Taylor was very conscious of his African heritage and was one of the delegates at the Pan-African Conference, which was held in London in 1900. He became friends with many important civil rights campaigners. Coleridge-Taylor wrote in his programme notes for *24 Negro Melodies* that: "What Brahms has done for the Hungarian folk music... and Grieg for the Norwegian, I have tried to do for these Negro Melodies." The piece is heavily influenced by African songs and those sung by enslaved Africans on the American plantations. Tragically, Samuel Coleridge-Taylor died of pneumonia in 1912 at the young age of 37.

Did you know?

Hiawatha's Wedding Feast was published by Novello, one of the most famous publishing companies of the time. Despite its success, Coleridge-Taylor did not make money from all its performances as he had sold it for a one-off payment.

Images of black people in art

From the 16th to 19th centuries, in the West, images of black men and women were created mostly by white artists and photographers. As a result, the way black people were portrayed was influenced by ideas held at the time about race and identity, which swayed the public towards certain attitudes and prejudices. Around the mid-20th century, the pictures began to change and become more positive.

Lowly positions

Many paintings, particularly those made during the time of the Transatlantic Slave Trade and the Imperial period (1830–1950s), when most of the countries in Africa were controlled by Europeans, show black people in low positions such as slaves, servants or 'clown-like' entertainers. However, there have also been paintings of individuals such as Ira Aldridge (see pages 14–15), Ignatius Sancho (a writer and early abolitionist campaigner), Mary Seacole (a nurse who went to the battlefields of the Crimea in the 1850s) and a photograph of Samuel Coleridge-Taylor (see pages 16–17), which showed the more positive side of contributions black people made in Britain.

▲ *Mary Seacole (1805–81) also appeared in some early photographs, like the one here.*

Abolitionist art

One of the iconic images associated with the campaign to abolish slavery was the kneeling African man holding up his chained hands with the words 'Am I not a man and a brother?' underneath. Although the abolitionist message was extremely important, and was a very effective way of getting support for the cause, the image of the African as a passive victim was also damaging. The image suggests that the enslaved Africans had accepted their position and had to be saved from slavery by the (white) abolitionists.

In recent times, a similar criticism has been made of the images that have been associated with Africa, especially those connected with famine and poverty. Often photographers and filmmakers show young children who are starving and living in terrible conditions as a way of gaining sympathy and funding for their relief. Although this helps raise money for those in need, it continues to reinforce the impression that Africans are victims.

▲ *These African-American minstrels are arriving in Bridgeton, New Jersey in 1942.*

After abolition

The stereotyping of black people as servants or entertainers continued after the abolition of slavery in Britain and the USA. Images of black people as minstrels (travelling performers) and tap dancers were later supplemented with images of black sports stars. This had a negative effect, suggesting it was all black people could do. It was not until the civil rights campaigns of the 1960s and the Black Consciousness movement – which argued that 'black is beautiful' – that positive images of black men and women in everyday life began to be produced.

▲ *The phrase 'Black is Beautiful' appears on a wall in Manchester, UK, in 1969.*

The Harlem Renaissance

In the United States during the 1920s, a movement of African-American artists, writers and musicians emerged that became known as the Harlem Renaissance. It was centred around the New York suburb of Harlem. Many African Americans had moved here from the poorer Southern states during the Great Migration of the 1890s to find work in the more prosperous North.

Langston Hughes

The poet, playwright and novelist Langston Hughes (1902–67) was one of the most famous writers of the Harlem Renaissance. His writing reflected the real experiences of African Americans – not only the harsh realities, but also the sense of community, love of music, and

Did you know?

The language spoken in Harlem, known as jive, was based on rhyme, slang and on the music of jazz. It has influenced rap and hip hop today.

▲ *This portrait of Langston Hughes was created c.1925 by Winold Reiss.*

laughter found in the homes of urban America. One of Hughes' best-known poems, *The Negro Speaks of Rivers*, was published in the NAACP (National Association for the Advancement of Colored People) magazine, *The Crisis*, in 1921. It spoke of the African heritage of black Americans.

Hughes was also very influenced by the jazz and blues music being played by black musicians in Harlem clubs. He wrote lyrics for the music of the great jazz bassist Charlie Mingus. He published 20 plays, 16 books of poetry, 3 collections of short stories, 2 novels and many other articles. Hughes died in 1967.

The Cotton Club

Activists such as W.E.B. du Bois criticised the Harlem Renaissance, arguing that writers like Hughes did not do enough to challenge negative stereotypes of African Americans. He was also concerned that at the Cotton Club, the most famous jazz club in Harlem, black performers played to an exclusively white audience. However, the positive impact of the Harlem Renaissance meant African-American writers and performers reached a much wider audience. Jazz greats such as Louis Armstrong, Duke Ellington, Billie Holiday and Ella Fitzgerald all began their careers during this period and have left a lasting legacy on music.

▲ *The front of the Cotton Club in Harlem, New York in the 1930s.*

First lady of song

Born in 1917, the jazz singer Ella Fitzgerald grew up in Yonkers, New York. After a troubled childhood, by 1934 she was entertaining a weekly audience at the Apollo Theater, going on to sing with bandleaders such as Chick Webb and Duke Ellington. In 1939, she led her own orchestra, recording 150 songs with it. Perhaps her greatest achievement was recording hundreds of songs for the Great American Song Book. Ella Fitzgerald won 13 Grammy Awards in a career spanning 59 years, making her one of the best-known singers in the world. She died in 1996.

▲ *Ella Fitzgerald performs on stage with Dizzy Gillespie in 1947.*

The London scene

As the blues, jazz and swing music became popular on both sides of the Atlantic, performers from the USA and the Caribbean travelled to Britain to play. Some of them, such as Adelaide Hall, decided to stay. The influx of Caribbean immigrants after World War II (1939–45) also brought a new musical style to Britain that was celebrated every year during the Notting Hill Carnival.

Adelaide Hall

Born in Brooklyn, New York in 1901, Adelaide Hall was a singer and songwriter who performed with some of the greatest jazz musicians of the era. She starred at the Cotton Club (see page 21) in Harlem, and recorded with Duke Ellington and his band. In 1938, she travelled to London to take a role in the musical *The Sun Never Sets* at the Theatre Royal in London.

Hall was so popular that she decided to stay in London and continue working there. By the early 1940s, she was one of the highest paid performers in the country. During her career, she made more than 70 records, and was the first black artist to be offered a radio contract by the BBC. She continued to sing well into her 80s, collaborating with such stars as Cab Calloway, Josephine Baker, Louis Armstrong and Lena Horne. Adelaide Hall died in 1993 at the age of 92 in London.

▲ *Adelaide Hall, dressed up for a performance in Paris, 1930.*

Calypso and carnival

The arrival of the ships, including the *Empire Windrush* in 1948, brought not only skilled workers, who provided labour for the new National Health Service and London Transport, but also talented musicians who brought a new sound to Britain – calypso. One of the passengers on the *Empire Windrush* was the Trinidadian musician, Aldwyn Roberts, known as 'Lord Kitchener', whose most famous songs included *London is the Place for Me* and *Cricket, Lovely Cricket*. The calypso style that he sang soon became very popular, particularly after the establishment of the Notting Hill Carnival in 1958. The music was played on steel drums and even at today's carnival, steel drum bands play calypso songs.

▲ *The Steel Pan Orchestra perform at the Notting Hill Carnival in London.*

▲ *Aldwyn Roberts, shortly before travelling to the USA to launch calypso in 1957.*

Did you know?

The Notting Hill Carnival was founded in 1958 by Claudia Jones, an African-American political activist and journalist. Outspoken about civil rights issues, she was deported from the USA for her activities in the American Communist party, and moved to Britain in 1955.

Writing in the civil rights era

The civil rights campaigns in the USA in the 1950s and 60s, which demanded equal rights for African Americans, were reflected in the literature of that time. The low position of African Americans had been highlighted by one of the most important writers of the 1940s, Richard Wright. He went on to exert a great influence over the writer most closely associated with the Civil Rights Movement – James Baldwin.

From *Native Son* to *Black Boy*

Richard Wright was born in Mississippi in 1908. His early years were scarred by hardship and poverty and he was unable to complete school. Wright often received punishments from his strict, religious grandmother, and he experienced racist abuse from his employers. However, by the age of 15, he had discovered a love of writing after gaining access to a library (by borrowing

◄ *The first edition jacket cover of* Native Son.

▲ *Richard Wright at his desk in 1948.*

a library card from a white man). His early experiences formed the basis of his writings as he reflected on the position of African Americans in society. In his novel *Native Son*, published in 1940, the main character, Bigger Thomas, described his frustration:

"We live here and they live there. We black and they white. They got things and we ain't. They do things and we can't. It's just like living in jail."

Wright published his semi-autobiographical book, *Black Boy*, in 1945, and both books became bestsellers. It was the first time an African-American writer had been recognised for exposing the reality of life in the black community to a wider audience. Wright moved to Paris in 1947, continuing to write and supporting emerging writers such as Gwendolyn Brooks and James Baldwin. He died in 1960 aged 52.

The Fire Next Time

The year after Wright moved to Paris, he was followed by the young African-American writer James Baldwin (1924–87), who was also moving to free himself from discrimination in the USA. Baldwin began writing novels and essays on the position of African Americans, arguing that things needed to be changed. In his most famous book, *The Fire Next Time*, Baldwin addresses his 14-year-old nephew, explaining how to overcome the prejudice and discrimination he faced. He argued that both blacks and whites needed to overcome their past in order to create a future for all. Baldwin returned to the USA

▲ *James Baldwin on the cover of* Time *magazine in May, 1963.*

to take part in the Civil Rights Movement. Here he wrote an essay called *No Name in the Street* about the assassinations of three of his friends: Medgar Evers (a civil rights activist), Martin Luther King Jr and Malcolm X.

Did you know?

The US Civil Rights Acts, which allowed African Americans to vote and outlawed discrimination, were passed in 1957 and 1964.

Motown

The Motown record label was founded by Berry Gordy in January 1959 in Detroit, Michigan, and became one of the most famous labels in the history of music. Its significance lay not only with the artists that it produced, but also in that it was an extremely successful organisation owned and run by African Americans. Its distinctive soul-pop music had a fresh energy and youthful sound that had not been heard before.

The Motown Sound

Motown artists included such stellar acts as Diana Ross and the Supremes, Marvin Gaye, Smokey Robinson and the Miracles, Stevie Wonder and the Jackson 5. Between 1961 and 1971, these artists dominated the music charts with over 100 top-ten singles. Motown had a team of songwriters and record producers who came up with what was called the Motown Sound. A typical song might feature tambourines, drums, moving bass lines and 'call and response' vocal harmonies, which originally came from the gospel music of African-American churches.

Political themes

Some Motown songs were about love but others spoke of political themes and the African-American experience of the 1960s and 70s. *Love Child*, a hit single from 1968 for Diana Ross and the Supremes, includes the line: *Started my life/ In an old, cold, run-down tenement slum/ My father left, he never even married Mom...*

Marvin Gaye's album *What's Going On?* from 1971 explored ecology, civil unrest in the US and the Vietnam War (1964–75), with songs like *Inner City Blues* and the title song: *Picket lines and picket signs/ Don't punish me with brutality/ Talk to me so you can see/ What's going on...*

▲ *Berry Gordy, founder of Motown – one of the most famous record labels of all time.*

The songs of Motown are still listened to and loved around the world.

▲ *(From right) Diana Ross and the Supremes; Florence Ballard and Mary Wilson.*

Civil rights

Berry Gordy also set up the Black Forum label to make and distribute recordings of civil rights leaders. In January 1963, on the day of the famous Civil Rights March on Washington, Motown released *The Great March to Freedom*, a recording of a Martin Luther King speech in Detroit. It also released material by Langston Hughes (see pages 20–21) and later, Stokely Carmichael of the radical Black Panther Party.

Smokey speaks

"I recognised the bridges that we crossed, the racial problems and the barriers that we broke down with music. I recognised that because I lived it. I would come to the South in the early days of Motown and the audiences would be segregated. Then they started to get the Motown music, and we would go back and the audiences were integrated and the kids were dancing together and holding hands."

Smokey Robinson – one of Motown's first artists, from the *Times Picayune Newspaper*, February 2009

Jimi Hendrix

IN DEPTH

If Motown represented the successful integration of African-American artists into the mainstream of popular music, the pioneering rock guitarist Jimi Hendrix showed the complexity of the issues of race, identity and music. Hendrix came from a mixed-heritage family, with roots in the white, African-American and Native American communities.

London calling

Jimi Hendrix grew up in Seattle, Washington and was given his first guitar at the age of five by his father. After an unsettled childhood, with Hendrix sometimes being looked after by his Cherokee grandmother, Hendrix joined the army in 1961 at the age of 19. On leaving the army, he became a session musician, performing with black artists such as Tina Turner and Little Richard. His career took a new direction when he moved to London and formed the Jimi Hendrix Experience with two white English musicians, Noel Redding and Mitch Mitchell.

The group's shows in London began to attract a large following, particularly after people learned of Jimi's charismatic performances, including setting his guitar on fire, which became one of his trademarks. The Jimi Hendrix Experience released their first album, *Are You Experienced*, in 1967, featuring innovative songs and charismatic performances. After a stunning concert at the Monterey Pop Festival in California, the band enjoyed great success in the USA.

▲ *Jimi Hendrix on stage at the Albert Hall in London, 1969.*

Black consciousness

Although he came from a mixed-heritage background and played music to a largely white audience, in the late 1960s Jimi Hendrix seemed to be more influenced by issues affecting the African-American community. This followed on from the assassination of Martin Luther King in 1968, when some African Americans moved away from the ideas of passive resistance and the

▲ *Members of the Black Panther Party on a protest march in New York, 1968.*

non-violence promoted by King, towards a more aggressive stance put forward by groups such as the Black Panther Party.

Gypsys and jazz

After the break up of the Jimi Hendrix Experience, Hendrix formed a new band of black performers, the Band of Gypsys, in 1970. He started to experiment more with jazz, working with black musicians such as trumpeter and composer Miles Davis. A recording of the live performance of the Band of Gypsys opens with a dedication from Hendrix to "all the soldiers fighting in Chicago and Milwaukee and New York. Oh, yes, and all the soldiers fighting and dying in Vietnam". This was a reference to both the race riots that had broken out in the USA and the concern that so many African-American soldiers were being killed in the war.

Yet for the most part, Hendrix did not seem overly interested in race issues. He even went as far as saying "Race isn't a problem in my world", which is maybe why he appealed to such a wide audience. Jimi Hendrix died of an accidental drug overdose in London in September 1970. He was 27 years old.

▼ *Miles Davis, shown here in around 1968, teamed up with Hendrix in the early 1970s.*

The reggae beat

In the 1970s, music played on British radio and TV shows such as *Top of the Pops* was becoming dominated by artists from the USA and Motown. By the mid-1970s, artists such as Stevie Wonder and Marvin Gaye began to be influenced by the new genre of funk, which would later evolve into disco. But in Britain, a new sound was emerging into the mainstream from the Caribbean – reggae.

Reggae comes to Britain

Labels such as Trojan and Island Records brought artists including Jimmy Cliff, Desmond Dekker and Bob Marley over to Britain. These artists were popular not only in the Caribbean communities, but across the country. The influence of reggae spread over to the spoken word with the emergence of the dub poets such as Linton Kwesi Johnson and Benjamin Zephaniah, who were inspired by the music and ideas behind reggae to create a new form of writing (see pages 32–33).

▲ *Jimmy Cliff (real name James Chambers) helped to bring reggae to the world.*

The roots of reggae

Although reggae is most closely associated with the Caribbean island of Jamaica, it has its roots in the music of Africa and the United States. The earliest form of reggae came from the sounds known as ska and rocksteady, but played at a much slower beat. This music was played by the original Jamaican skinheads or 'rudeboys' in the dance halls and was soon picked up by the Caribbean communities in Britain.

The next phase saw the emergence of 'roots reggae', the sound most closely associated with Bob Marley. The lyrics in roots reggae songs were more religious and linked with the Rastafari movement, a religious movement that came out of Jamaica.

Marley and the Wailers

Bob Marley came from a mixed-heritage background (white British father, black Jamaican mother). In the late 1960s he began playing music with a group known as the Wailers. Their first album, *Catch a Fire*, was released in 1973 –followed with a tour of Britain. Their second album – *Burnin'* – featured the singles, *I Shot the Sheriff* and *Get Up, Stand Up*.

Marley's lyrics became more political, with an awareness of the continuing hardship faced by people of African heritage around the world. The album *Survival* from 1979 had a number of songs that spoke of the challenges Africa faced, and Marley became closely involved in the anti-apartheid movement that fought racial discrimination in South Africa. In 1981, at the age of 36, Bob Marley died of cancer.

▲ *Bob Marley performs with his band, the Wailers, in Hamburg, Germany, 1976.*

Did you know?

Rastafarians believe that Africa is their spiritual home and that Haile Selassie, the last Emperor of Ethiopia, was their god. Selassie lived in exile in Bath, UK, from 1936–41 after the Italian dictator Mussolini invaded Ethiopia.

▲ *Emperor Haile Selassie arrives at Southampton, UK, in 1936.*

Dub poets

A type of performance poetry, dub poetry uses spoken words in a rhythmic pattern, a bit like chanting. It began in the Caribbean in the 1970s, when poets started speaking words over reggae music rhythms. Two dub poets – Linton Kwesi Johnson and Benjamin Zephaniah – have made this style popular in Britain.

Linton Kwesi Johnson

▲ *Linton Kwesi Johnson performs on stage in Amsterdam, 1980.*

The original 'reggae poet', Linton Kwesi Johnson (LKJ) arrived in London from Jamaica in 1963 at 11 years old. He joined the youth wing of the British Black Panther Party, and at school in Tulse Hill he started to write and perform poetry. In 1974, he released his first collection of poetry, *Voices of the Living and the Dead*, which spoke of the discrimination that many black Britons faced during a time of rising racial tension. LKJ's most famous work – *Inglan Is A Bitch* – was published in 1980, shortly before the Brixton riots broke out. It speaks of the frustration that many black Britons faced working long hours, receiving low wages and experiencing racism.

▲ *Cars were upturned and fires started during the Brixton riots in south London.*

LKJ was influenced by dub musicians of the Caribbean. Dub musicians took out the lyrics and melody from reggae songs to allow vocalists or 'toasters' to rap over the top, and LKJ was the first poet to use this approach in Britain. He released a number of albums where he spoke his poetry over music provided by Dennis Bovell, his musical collaborator. In 2003, Linton Kwesi Johnson was awarded an Honorary Fellowship from Goldsmiths College for his contribution to contemporary British writing. He continues to perform today.

Benjamin Zephaniah

One of Britain's most popular poets, Benjamin Zephaniah, has also been an activist and campaigner for human rights for many years. He has published and performed his poetry around the world. Zephaniah grew up in Birmingham in the 1960s. He struggled with dyslexia at school and left at the age of 13. He moved to London and started to publish his poetry, which he was determined would reach as wide an audience as possible. He performed on the radio and televison, in theatres and on the street in order to get his message across. Zephaniah's poetry touches on many different subjects ranging from the death of Stephen Lawrence (a black teenager who was killed in a racist attack in London in 1993), to race riots and football.

In 2003, Benjamin Zephaniah rejected an OBE (Order of the British Empire), an award given by the Queen. The reasons he gave included his rejection of any association with the British Empire, which reminded him of 'thousands of years of brutality' – a reference to the Transatlantic Slave Trade, for which there has been no official apology from the British government.

▲ *Benjamin Zephaniah, shown above in 2003, has also published several books for young adults.*

Punk and two-tone

In the late 1970s, punk (a loud, aggressive form of rock) and two-tone styles dominated British music. Many of the leading punk artists including Joe Strummer of The Clash were heavily influenced by reggae, while many of the two-tone bands, such as The Specials and The Beat, featured black and white musicians playing together.

▲ *One of the Rock Against Racism events at Brockwell Park near Brixton, south London.*

Rock Against Racism

One of the most important events of the punk era was the series of concerts called Rock Against Racism in 1978. The concerts were organised by the Anti-Nazi League, which was concerned about the rise in support for the racist National Front, and by comments made by famous musicians including Eric Clapton and David Bowie that were seen as racist. Over 80,000 people came to Victoria Park in London to see bands such as The Clash and Steel Pulse. Rock Against Racism was seen as a significant contribution to the defeat of the National Front.

Two-Tone

The music of two-tone was heavily influenced by ska and rocksteady, which had come out of Jamaica in the 1960s and been taken up by the Mod movement. Two-tone emerged in the 1980s with bands like The Specials, The Selector, Madness and The Beat, many of whom were made up of black and white musicians. The audiences that they played for were multi-cultural too – even the clothes and images associated with two-tone were black and white. The signature track of the

▲ *The Specials on a tour of the USA in 1980.*

two-tone era was *Ghost Town* by The Specials, which spoke of the desperate times that Britain was facing in the early 1980s, with high unemployment and rising racial tension. The single hit number one in the pop charts the day after race riots broke out across the UK.

Shared attitudes

There was a strong connection between the ideas and attitudes of Punk with the Rastafarians making reggae music in Jamaica. Both were concerned with the isolation and discrimination against which they had to fight, and the desire for freedom and respect. Some punk bands, such as The Clash, toured with reggae bands such as Steel Pulse. In 1977, Bob Marley released a track as a B-side called *Punky Reggae Party* to celebrate the coming together of the two genres.

▼ *Bob Marley released* Punky Reggae Party *on the Jamming single.*

From hip hop to dubstep

Although hip hop is most closely associated with the USA, its origin lies in Jamaica, and it has a small but significant place in British music. When the UK hip hop scene emerged in the late 1980s, another genre was hitting the London clubs from Jamaica – drum and bass (DnB). Dubstep has evolved out of DnB, with its origins in the dub reggae of the 1970s and 1980s.

The origins of hip hop

DJ Kool Herc is credited with originating hip hop in the early 1970s, when he set up his two turntables and a microphone, played beats and rapped over them. The dancers, known as B-boys (short for break-boys), and the graffiti art of the Bronx that accompanied the hip hop scene, combined to make up the four elements of hip hop: emceeing, DJing, breakdancing and graffiti.

▲ *Snoop Dogg, part of the West Coast rap scene that grew during the mid-to-late 1990s.*

By the 1990s, hip hop had spawned a wide range of varieties from the East Coast sounds of Wu Tang Clan and Notorious BIG, to the West Coast artists such as NWA and Snoop Dogg, the latter gaining a reputation as 'gangsta rap'. Many of the hip hop artists spoke of the struggles that

▲ *DJ Kool Herc (real name Clive Campbell) pioneered the use of twin turntables.*

▲ *LTJ Bukem (real name Danny Williamson) led the way in drum and bass developments in the UK.*

they faced in the ghettos, such as the poverty of their neighbourhoods and overcoming the influences of gang and drug cultures. The UK hip hop scene emerged in the mid-1980s, with artists such as Rodney P and Roots Manuva preferring to tell their tales of growing up on the streets of Britain. Many of the British artists were influenced by the sounds of reggae, unlike those in the USA, where the influence of funk and disco were much stronger.

Jungle and dubstep

The early DnB scene in Britain was also known as jungle. This came out of the inner cities of London, Bristol and Birmingham,

areas that have had a multi-cultural population for many years. The 'junglists' were also influenced by the reggae sound systems coming out of Jamaica, with Shy FX's *Original Nuttah* having a lot of commercial success. DnB artists such as Goldie, LTJ Bukem, Fabio and Grooverider have moved into the mainstream, with the latter duo hosting a regular show on BBC Radio. In the 21st century, the most recent style to emerge – dubstep – has seen a return to the influence of dub reggae merged with UK garage music sounds, featuring heavy bass lines and electronic instruments.

Contemporary artists, musicians and writers

Black artists, writers, musicians and actors have made incredibly strong and enduring contributions to world culture. Following civil rights victories made during the 20th century, new opportunities for people of African origin are greater than ever. As society becomes increasingly diverse, both positive and negative issues are being represented in the creative work of black performers.

Multi-cultural society

The diverse nature of modern society, particularly in Britain and the USA, has inspired many to reflect on what it means to be a black Briton or an African American in the 21st century. Not only are people from different backgrounds living in

▲ *Tinie Tempah (centre) with Krept & Konan at the 2013 MOBO Awards.*

the same areas, but also individuals and families themselves may be a mixture of African, European, Asian and other backgrounds.

Many artists have spoken of their multiple identities as being a great influence on their work. British artist, Chris Ofili, sites his experiences visiting Zimbabwe as a young man, the hip hop that he listens to, and living in culturally diverse London, as all being influences on his artwork. Others have been influenced by the ideas of the Black Panther Party or Black Consciousness, or the jazz, blues, reggae, Motown, soul, R&B, funk, disco or hip hop that they listened to.

Black stars

Actors such as Will Smith and Samuel L. Jackson have starred in and helped create blockbuster films, while writers such as Zadie Smith, Andrea Levy, Toni Morrison and Pulitzer Prize winner Alice Walker (who wrote *The Color Purple*) have published bestsellers that are read around the globe. The talented genius of internationally famous musicians such as Aretha Franklin

▲ *Will Smith has appeared in successful films, including* I Am Legend *(2007).*

and Michael Jackson has been an inspiration to millions of people. Black artists continue to speak to their audiences in unique and varied ways. Their voices are heard everywhere.

▲ *Author, Zadie Smith, is most famous for her novel* White Teeth.

Michael Jackson

Launching his career with his brothers in the Jackson 5 at just six years old, singer, dancer and songwriter Michael Jackson went on to become one of the most influential and successful solo recording artists in history. He had 17 number one singles and won 13 Grammy Awards. His album *Thriller* from 1982 is the best-selling album of all time. Michael Jackson died in 2009.

Timeline – Arts and Music

1750–1800 The height of the Transatlantic Slave Trade – millions of Africans were transported to the Americas. During this time they tried to preserve their songs, dances and traditions

1773 Phillis Wheatley's *Poems on Various Subjects, Religious and Moral* published in London

1789 Equiano published his autobiography, *The Interesting Narrative of Gustavus Vassa* or *Olaudah Equiano, the African*

1807 Ira Aldridge, actor, born. The abolition of the slave trade

1831 Mary Prince's autobiography published

1833 Ira Aldridge performed Othello at the Theatre Royal, London. The abolition of slavery in parts of the British Empire

1849 'Blind Tom' Bethune, the child musical prodigy, was born

1865 The abolition of slavery in the United States of America

1898 Samuel Coleridge-Taylor wrote *Hiawatha's Wedding Feast*

1900 The first Pan-African Conference in London

1920s The Harlem Renaissance – black writers and jazz musicians flourished in Harlem, New York

1921 Langston Hughes' poem *The Negro Speaks of Rivers* published in *The Crisis*, the magazine of the NAACP

1940 Richard Wright published *Native Son*

1945 Richard Wright published *Black Boy*

1948 The *Empire Windrush* docked in London, bringing a number of Caribbean musicians to England

1958 The first Notting Hill Carnival

1959 Motown Records formed by Berry Gordy in Detroit

1963 Motown released a recording of Martin Luther King on the day of the March on Washington. James Baldwin published his essay *The Fire Next Time*

1967 The Jimi Hendrix Experience released their first album *Are You Experienced?*

1973 Bob Marley and the Wailers released their first album *Catch A Fire*

1974 *Voices of the Living and the Dead* released by Linton Kwesi Johnson, the first dub poet

1978 Rock Against Racism concerts held in east London and Manchester

1979 *Rapper's Delight*, the first successful hip hop track is released

1981 The Brixton riots set off a chain of 'race riots' around the UK. *Ghost Town* by The Specials goes to Number 1

2003 Benjamin Zephaniah rejects the offer of an OBE; Chris Ofili represented Britain at the Venice Biennale

2004 Andrea Levy won the Orange Prize for Fiction for *Small Island*

2010 Will Smith produced the film *Karate Kid*

2012 Architect David Adjaye heads the Powerlist of 100 top role models in the UK

2013 Tinie Tempah wins MOBO Award for the best UK Hip Hop/Grime Act

2013 Malorie Blackman becomes Children's Laureate

2013 Oprah Winfrey is ranked number one most influential celebrity by Forbes

2014 *12 Years A Slave*, directed by Steve McQueen, wins three Academy Awards, a Golden Globe Award and a BAFTA

2014 Rihanna wins CFDA Fashion Icon Award

Websites and Bibliography

Websites

http://www.pbs.org/wnet/slavery/ experience/education/history2.html
Excellent overview of the connection between slavery and African music.

http://chevalierdesaintgeorges.homes tead.com/index.html Comprehensive website with articles about black composers and musicians.

http://www.jbhe.com/features/59 _richardwright.html Essay about the significance of Richard Wright with extracts from his books.

http://www.100greatblack britons.co m Website where you can find biographies of many black artists, writers and musicians.

http://www.bbc.co.uk/history/ british /abolition/ black_imagery_gallery.shtml
Representations of black people in art.

http://www.benjaminzephaniah.com
Benjamin Zephaniah's website.

Bibliography

Beckford R, *Jesus dub: theology, music and social change,* Routledge, 2006

Dawson A, *Mongrel Nation: diasporic culture and the making of postcolonial Britain,* University of Michigan Press, 2007

Donnell A, and Lawson Welsh S, *The Routledge Reader in Caribbean Literature,* Routledge, 1996

Jackson Fosset J, and Tucker J, *Race consciousness: African American studies for the new century,* New York University Press, 1997

Kato M, *From kung fu to hip hop: globalization, revolution and popular culture,* SUNY Press, 2007

Mahon M, *Right to rock: the black Rock Coalition and the cultural politics of race,* Duke University Press, 2004

Proctor J, *Writing black Britain 1948-1998, An Interdisciplinary Anthology,* Manchester University Press, 2000

Smith S, *Dancing in the street: Motown and the cultural politics of Detroit,* Harvard University Press, 1999

Southern E, *The Music of black Americans, A History,* W W Norton & Co., 1997

Stallabrass J, *High art lite: British Art in the 1990s,* Verso, 1999

Glossary

Abolitionist
Someone who wanted to abolish the slavery of black Africans.

Americas
The word used to describe all the lands of both North and South America.

Autistic
Used to describe someone with autism, a development disorder that makes it difficult to communicate with others.

Black Panther Party
A civil rights group in the USA in the 1960s and 1970s. It was prepared to use violence to get what it wanted.

Blues
A style of music, usually sung, that developed from the songs of black slaves in the southern USA in the mid-19th century.

Brixton riots
Three days of rioting in April 1981 in Brixton, south London where a crowd of mostly young black men attacked buildings, cars and the police. The riots were a reaction to the poor jobs and opportunities for the black community.

Caesar, Julius
He was a politician and general in the army of ancient Rome.

Calypso
A type of Caribbean song, with a syncopated rhythm.

Civil rights
The rights of all people to social and political freedom.

Civil unrest
A public demonstration of violence by three people or more.

Cotton Club
A famous jazz nightclub in Harlem, New York, USA.

Crimea
Part of modern-day Ukraine.

Discrimination
Unfair treatment of a person or group because of their race, sex or beliefs.

Dubstep
A type of dance music.

Dyslexia
A learning difficulty which affects reading and writing skills.

Equal rights
The same rights for everyone, regardless of their wealth or the colour of their skin.

Griot
A traditional singer/songwriter from West Africa.

Immigrant
Someone who moves to another country to settle.

Jazz
A musical style that developed from the blues (see above) in the early 20th century.

Lyrics
The words that make up a song.

Mixed race
The child of parents of different races, for instance a white British man and a black African woman.

National Front
A British right-wing political party with strong, racist beliefs.

Pan-African
Of, or for, all Africans, including those who live in countries other than those on the African continent.

Plantation
A large farm where crops are raised.

Prejudice
An opinion or dislike formed against something or someone.

Race riot
A riot caused by hatred for people of other races living in the same community.

Rapping
Chanting repeated words or rhyming words to strong rhythmic music.

Shackles
A metal fastening used to keep someone captive.

Slavery
When someone is forced to work for another person and loses all of their freedom and rights.

Transatlantic Slave Trade
The name given to the enslavement and forced removal of millions of Africans from Africa to the Americas between the 16th and 19th centuries.

Transportation
To send a criminal abroad to a foreign country as a punishment. They had to work for a set amount of time, or even for the rest of their lives.

Vietnam War
A war fought by the US in Vietnam between 1965 and 1973.

Index

These are the lists of contents for the titles in *Black History*:

African Empires
Introduction
African Empires
Ta-Seti and Ancient Egypt
The Kingdom of Ta-Seti
Ancient Ghana
What was life like in Kumbi Saleh?
The Empire of Mali
Mansa Musa and the pilgrimage to Mecca
The Empire of Songhai
A rough guide to Timbuktu
The Kigdom of Benin
Living in Benin
Great Zimbabwe
Who built Great Zimbabwe?
The Europeans arrive
African resistance
A timeline of African empires
Websites and Bibliography

Africa and the Slave Trade
Introduction
Slavery around the world
West Africa at the time of the Transatlantic Slave Trade
The start of the Transatlantic Slave Trade
Britain and the triangular trade
Capture
Elmina
The Middle Passage
Olaudah Equiano
Arriving in the Americas
Sugar!
What was it like to work on the plantations?
What was it like to live on the plantations?
Mary Prince
How did enslaved Africans maintain their culture?
What was the legacy of slavery for Africa?
A timeline of the Transatlantic Slave Trade
Websites and Bibliography

Resistance and Abolition
Introduction
Resistance in Africa
Resistance on the slave ships
The Amistad
Resistance on the plantations
Slave revolts
Nanny of the Maroons
Toussaint L'Ouverture's rebellion
Abolition
Africans in Britain
Olaudah Equiano the Abolitionist
Society for the Abolition of the Slave Trade
Am I not a man and a brother?
The Abolition Acts
Elizabeth Heyrick
The legacy of the slave trade
Timeline – Resistance and Abolition
Websites and Bibliography

Civil Rights and Equality
Introduction
Nineteenth-century radicals
The Pan-African Conference 1900
John Archer
World War I
Race Riots
The League of Coloured Peoples
World War II
Windrush generation
Claudia Jones
Roots of the Civil Rights Movement
Martin Luther King and civil rights
The civil rights laws
The rise of Black Power
Race in the USA today
Race relations in the UK
Timeline – Civil Rights and Equality
Websites and Bibliography

Arts and Music
Introduction
The music of Africa
The impact of slavery
The actor – Ira Aldridge
The composer – Samuel Coleridge-Taylor
Images of black people in art
The Harlem Renaissance
The London scene
Writing in the civil rights era
Motown
Jimi Hendrix
The reggae beat
Dub poets
Punk and two-tone
From hip hop to dubstep
Contemporary artists, musicians and writers
Timeline – Arts and Music
Websites and Bibliography

Community and Identity
Introduction
Black Britons and African Americans
Multiculturalism
Community leaders
Diane Abbott and Condoleezza Rice
Flash points
Overcoming barriers
Celebrating black culture
Black people in the media
Sporting achievements
Sport and community
Tackling gang culture
The legacy of Rodney King
Stephen Lawrence
Black role models
Diverse future
Timeline – Community and Identity
Websites and Bibliography